The Priceless Gift
Stories of Christmas

The Priceless Gift

Stories of Christmas

Meredith Woods Potter

4:13 Publishing, in partnership with
Masterful Person Company Publishing
mpcpublishing.com

ISBN: 97986850865

Library of Congress Control Number: 2024919930

Second Edition.

Typeface: Garamond 14p.

Cover design and illustration by Roane Furlong.

Table of Contents

A *N*ote to the *R*eader

This small book of sermons was compiled as a Christmas gift for my grandchildren and great-grandchildren. I hope that these stories will remind them that the greatest Christmas gift they will ever receive is God's gift of the Christ child to them and to all of humankind. These sermons were selected from nearly twenty years of preaching on Christmas morning at St. Gregory's Episcopal Church, Deerfield, Illinois, where I hung out in retirement. With the exception of the last sermon, "The Cosmic Christmas," which is based on the opening sentences of the Gospel of John, all sermons are reflections on the traditional Christmas readings: Isaiah 9:2-7 and Luke 2: 1-14 (15-20).

~Meredith Woods Potter

I Love to Tell the Story

For the past week a hymn has been bubbling into my consciousness from somewhere deep within me. It's not exactly a Christmas hymn, although it certainly bears a Christmas message. It's not even a hymn in our Episcopal hymnal, so I've wondered why it seems to have settled in my unconscious heart. Perhaps some of you, like me, sang this hymn as a child:

"I love to tell the story of unseen things above, of Jesus and his glory, of Jesus and his love. . ." *

As I began to pay attention to what my heart seemed to be singing, I realized that I really do love to *tell the story* - the story of God's love in the gift of the Christ child - and particularly the Christmas story as Luke tells it in today's

Gospel. I also love to *hear the story* - in the hymns we sing on this day, in today's Gospel when it is proclaimed by our deacon or narrated by a child in the Christmas pageant. And I love *to see the story* - when I gaze upon our manger at the front of our altar, or the smaller version displayed in my home. But most of all I love *to experience the story* - as we did last Sunday during the Christmas pageant, as our children helped us experience Jesus' birth, by re-enacting the roles of St. Nicholas, Mary, Joseph, Gabriel, angels, shepherds, sheep, and the brand-new baby Jesus, portrayed by one of our youngest and newest members of the body of Christ.

This year, several church members and I experienced today's Gospel in yet another very special way. We traveled to St. Ignatius Church in Antioch to participate in a live nativity. Every member of that congregation took part in some aspect of the story - centurions demanding that we pay to travel the Roman road, the rector portraying a poor beggar, a choir of angels singing as we went along our route, until finally we found ourselves at the manger where two youths portrayed a somewhat frightened and astonished Mary and Joseph. It was all very real, including a real camel, several sheep, and a young donkey for Mary to ride on. In spite of frigid weather, it was obvious that every participant loved telling their part of the story, and I drove home feeling as if I had been transported into a different time and space - transported into the events of this morning's Gospel.

Throughout history - before we began to tell and hear and see and experience the story of Jesus' birth - the story had already been foretold by the prophets. Our reading from Isaiah (*Isaiah 52: 7-10*) set the stage for the "good news" that was to come. With their city and temple destroyed and after years of wandering in exile, the people of Israel had become convinced that God had not only abandoned the Holy City, God had abandoned the chosen people as well. And so it was with special joy and expectation that they heard the messenger proclaim God's impending return to Zion, the announcement of God's salvation, and the good news that "your God reigns." Isaiah promises that something special will happen to Jerusalem, "that all the ends of the earth shall see the salvation of our God." Isaiah's prophecy prepares the people of Israel for the Incarnation; Isaiah prepares the world for the story to come.

Isaiah had the respect and authority of the people, so they could believe in the future that God had promised. Yet the first ones to tell the world what they had seen and what they had experienced were unlikely messengers.

In spite of the romantic notions we Christians have about shepherds - a notion reinforced by portraits of God as "the good Shepherd," and seeing our adorable young children dressed up as shepherds for the Christmas pageant - shepherds were not sweet or innocent like our children. Palestinian shepherds lived out-of-doors most of the time, pursued a nomadic lifestyle and were paid extremely poor wages. Even though Abraham, Moses and David are all described as keeping sheep, by the time of Jesus shepherding had become relegated to the lowest ranks of society. Shepherds were smelly, unruly, uneducated, ruffians. They had the reputation of being crooks, hustlers, liars, degenerates, and thieves. They were so unreliable that their testimony was not admissible in court; they were not even permitted to observe the Jewish Sabbath, because they were considered to be ritually unclean. A Jewish rabbi once commented that no position in the world at that time was more despised than that of the shepherd. And yet the angel of the Lord chose these outcast peasants to become the first witnesses - to be the first to tell the story of Christ's birth.

It's rather amazing that anyone believed the story they had to tell, and yet it was no accident that Luke reports the story of the shepherds (*Luke 2: 1-20*). The shepherds' prominent role in proclaiming the "Good News" reminds us that when God acts in this world, God often acts through people who have no status in society - people whom the world considers to be unimportant, unworthy, and even unbelievable. And yet it was those downtrodden, woebegone, poor shepherds who became the first to tell the story. And throughout history the story has been told again and again by people whose only credentials have been their love to tell the story: the story they have seen and heard and experienced of the Lord Jesus coming into their lives!

And today it is our turn to tell the story. The hymn reminds us why we need to tell it again and again and again:

"I love to tell the story, for some have never heard
   the message of salvation from God's own holy word.
I love to tell the story, for those who know it best
   seem hungering and thirsting to hear it like the rest;
And when in scenes of glory I sing the new, new song,
'Twill be the old, old story that I have loved so long."

God calls you and me to continue to proclaim the good news of great joy to all people: "That unto us is born this day in the city of David a Savior, who is the Messiah, the Lord." *(Isaiah 9:6)* And so today, God is counting on you and on me to find someone who may never have heard or seen or experienced the true meaning of Christmas and tell them "the old, old story of Jesus and His love."

Words were first written by an evangelist Katherine Hankey as a poem in 1866. The words were then set to music by William G. Fischer in 1869. Although the hymn appears in over one thousand hymnals, it does not appear in any Episcopal hymnal publication. Words and music are now in the public domain.

Christmas morning 2010

The Choice, the Decision, the Gift

(Joseph's Story)

Joseph kicked his sandals into the sandy soil as he trudged along the road to Bethlehem. He could see the town in the distance, but he figured it would be at least another hour before they reached their destination. Even the donkey had grown tired, and so Joseph gave a tug on its rope to keep the animal moving. He turned his head to look back at Mary. She looked so uncomfortable, yet she managed a faint smile. Joseph couldn't help but wonder what he had gotten himself into. He had fallen so in love with

Mary – her gentle ways, her quick wit, her beauty. He had really been looking forward to their marriage and life together; but then so unexpectedly had come her announcement. At first he just didn't believe it. How could she possibly be pregnant?

And her explanation sounded far-fetched and impossible.

Beside himself as to what to do, Joseph had gone to his father for advice. He had expected his father to tell him to cancel the engagement quietly to avoid public humiliation for Mary and her problem. But his father, a devout Jew and a very thoughtful man, had surprised him. He had suggested to Joseph that he had a choice and a decision to make. He had told his son that Jewish law certainly permitted Joseph to break the engagement, but that there was another option. And then surprisingly, his father had asked Joseph two questions: How much did he love Mary? And how much did he trust God?

Those two questions had sent Joseph's mind whirling. Could he really believe Mary and the truth of what she had shared? If he could bring himself to trust that this child in Mary's womb was from God, then he loved Mary all the more for her faith, and her trust, and her courage. And so Joseph did indeed have a choice to make, and with that choice would come a decision that would not only affect Mary, but would affect his own life forever.

As Joseph struggled with what to do, he had fallen into a restless sleep. An angel of the Lord had appeared to him in a dream and had confirmed everything that Mary had shared with him. The angel had told Joseph that the child would fulfill the words spoken by the prophet: "The virgin shall conceive and bear a son, and they shall name him Immanuel, which means 'God is with us'" (*Isaiah 7:14*). When Joseph had awakened, his mind was made up. He had made his decision. He would choose to trust God's promise; he would marry his beloved Mary.

But Joseph was not only a devout Jew, he was also subject to the laws of the Roman authorities who occupied the land. And Caesar Augustus, the Roman Emperor, had decreed that all residents of the occupied territories would have to return to their birthplace to participate in a census. And so Joseph had to take Mary and travel from Nazareth to his family's hometown, which was Bethlehem. He had been forced to delay the trip, because Mary had gone to visit her cousin Elizabeth and had not returned until somewhat late in her pregnancy. And that's why on this night Joseph found himself exhausted, worried, and hurrying to find lodging in Bethlehem.

Joseph's uncle had given him the name of an inn where they could stay, but the town was bursting with other travelers who had also come to be counted, and his uncle's friend had no rooms by the time Joseph and Mary had arrived. And so with Mary about to give birth, the couple frantically had gone from one inn to another. Joseph had despaired of ever finding a place for them to spend the night - a place for Mary to give birth. But then finally a sympathetic innkeeper had offered them the most unlikely of rooms - a cave where sheep were housed. Joseph had done the best he could to turn the makeshift quarters into a somewhat comfortable room for Mary. He had fashioned a bed of straw for her; he had fetched water; he had hung their small lamp; he had fashioned a simple meal for them.

And now he was holding the new baby – the God child. Joseph thought his heart would burst with love and joy. Shepherds had learned of the birth and began to arrive to pay their respects and to give glory to God. The word spread to the village and now villagers were also coming in and out, expressing their joy. But Joseph paid them almost no attention, for his thoughts were consumed with "what ifs": what if he had dismissed Mary and refused to marry her; what if he hadn't dreamed of the angel's visit and been reminded of the prophet's words of this miraculous birth that was to come; what if he had failed to say "yes" to God; what if Mary had not said "yes" to God. But none of those "what ifs" mattered now. God *had* been with them; and God *had* given Joseph the greatest task of all - to help his beloved Mary parent the God child. And so Joseph offered his own prayers; he prayed that as a husband and parent God would give him strength, and courage, and wisdom. But most of all his heart was filled with prayers of joy and wonder and thanksgiving.

As we engage the Christmas story once again this morning, we too have a choice and a decision to make. "For unto us a child is born; unto us a son is given" (*Isaiah 9:6*). Will we *choose* to accept God's precious gift to us? Will we *decide* to take Jesus into our hearts, just as Joseph decided to trust God and take the God child into his heart? Today our hearts can be that birthing place where God's greatest gift of love can find a home. Then God's promise will come true for each of us; and we too will experience the meaning of Immanuel: God will be with us, now and forever.

Christmas morning 2011

No Room at the Inn

Mary tried to shift into a more comfortable position on the donkey's back. Her whole body ached, and no matter how she tried to position herself in the seat that Joseph had built for her, the sharp pains had begun to surge through her body. Joseph had been so attentive, stopping frequently so she could stretch and walk a bit during the journey, but he also had been intent on pushing ahead steadily toward their destination. And now she was glad he had been persistent. Her pains were coming more and more frequently. It was a good thing they could see Bethlehem ahead. Mary wanted to get settled comfortably in the inn, for she was sure that the baby would be born tonight.

As they reached a small lodging on the outskirts of town, Joseph placed his calloused hand on hers. "We'll soon be settled," he whispered. "Why don't you just stay there on the donkey? I'll only be a moment." But when he returned his eyes were downcast. He could hardly look at Mary. "They don't have any room here," he muttered. "We'll have to go on to the inn in town." As they trudged toward the center of Bethlehem, Joseph blamed himself for not having arrived a day or two earlier. He should have known that there would be many travelers like themselves, coming to Bethlehem to register and pay their taxes.

And now as the innkeeper shakes his head, Joseph becomes not only frustrated but worried about what to do now. Mary, too, is concerned as the pains are coming more and more frequently. What are they to do? The innkeeper, noticing Mary's condition and the couple's distress, responds, "I don't have a room to offer, but there is a small stable in back. You're welcome to stay there. You'll find water which I put out for the animals and the straw is soft and will keep you warm."

Joseph reaches up and puts his arms around Mary, lifting her from her seat on the donkey's back, and then tenderly carries his wife into the stable. As he busily tries to create a bed of the straw, his thoughts turn to the impending birth. How can they manage? Mary's thoughts are also about the baby. God has given her such an important role in God's gift to the world, and yet now she feels very alone. How can she carry out God's plan when she doesn't even have a proper place to prepare for the birth? As the couple settles into their makeshift accommodations, Mary and Joseph look at each other in silence. They share the same unspoken thoughts: "Why wasn't there a room for us? Couldn't God have found a better place for God's Son to be born?"

The Church has always seen in today's reading from Isaiah (*Isaiah 52:7-10*) the foretelling of the coming of the Christ child. When Isaiah made his prophecy, the people of Israel had been experiencing dark and difficult times. The kingdom had been divided; the Northern kingdom had fallen to Assyria and Judah was being threatened. But these dark times were about to change, proclaimed the prophet. Soon there would be joy and optimism again. For soon the Child of hope would be born. This Child would be called Wonderful Counselor, Mighty God, Everlasting Father, Prince of Peace - the attributes we Christians ascribe to the Christ child. Isaiah prophesies that this child of hope will be Emmanuel - God with us. He will be King. And yet how unexpected that this kingship is inaugurated with a manger for his throne - because there was no place for the Child of hope - no room in the inn.

Today there is still "no room in the inn" - no place for Jesus in many parts of the world. Two-thirds of the earth's people have not heard, or have not believed, the story of the Messiah's birth - the story we have gathered to hear again this morning. It is now more than 2000 years since the Messiah's birth, and we can only wonder why there seems to be no room for the Wonderful Counselor of Isaiah's prophecy at world summits when nations gather to talk about world hunger, the AIDS pandemic, and educational opportunities for the world's poorest children. Why did there seem to be no place for the Prince of Peace when our government deliberated and authorized the sending of 30,000 of our young men and women into Afghanistan? Why has the world been unable to find lodging for the Child of hope in Iraq, Palestine, Pakistan, Rwanda, Somalia, Angola, Sudan, Liberia, and Burundi? - places where there has been no peace this past year. Perhaps it is because there has been no place for the Prince of Peace.

And yet the Child of hope brings hope to the world; we just need to find room in the world for the Christ child. The innkeeper had no room in his inn, but he did provide what he had - he provided his stable. He brought them water and straw and swaddling clothes for the new infant. He did what he could. And the Child of hope can bring hope to the world if you and I do what we can to make a place for the Christ child. Perhaps like the innkeeper we might provide the stable - or perhaps we might even BE the stable!!! Patrick Murfin in his book "*We Build Temples in the Heart*" wrote a poem titled "Let us be that Stable." He writes in part:

> "*Today, let us be that stable,*
> *let us be the place that welcomes at last the*
> *weary and rejected, the pilgrim stranger,*
> *the coming life.*

*Let our outstretched arms be a manger so that the
infant hope, swaddled in love, may have a place to lie." *

As we engage the Christmas message, let us
become the stable. It matters not that we may
feel inadequate. That first stable was inadequate.
But it served the purpose and shepherds and
angels and wise men from throughout the world
came to that stable to rejoice and give glory to
God. Today our hearts can be the birthing place
where God's greatest gift of love can find a
home. Come, let us be the stable for the Child of
hope. Come, let us make room in our hearts and
lives for the Christ child. Come, let us adore
him!!

Patrick Murfin. We Build Temples in the Heart: Side by Side We Gather (Skinner House Books, 2004.) At the time of publication, the author was active in civil rights, peace and labor movements, was serving as president of the Interfaith Council for Social Justice, and was a member of the Congregational Unitarian Church of Woodstock, Illinois.

Christmas morning 2009

Peace on Earth

(The Young Shepherd's Story)

The young boy crouched over the fire and rubbed his hands together. It was his first night tending the sheep by himself. He had begged his father to let him take responsibility for the flock now that he was twelve years old and had become a man, according to Jewish tradition. But in the dark and cold desert night the young boy didn't feel quite so grown up. In fact, if he had to admit it, he was a bit lonely and frightened. As he gazed into the desert night, he could just make out another small fire in the distance – probably the neighboring shepherd, trying to keep warm in the desert night, just like him. Overcome by the need for human companionship, he began to walk toward the fire.

As he approached the neighboring fire, he could tell that something was going on. A number of shepherds seemed to be gathering around some stranger. The boy edged closer in time to hear the stranger say, "Do not be afraid; for see – I am bringing you good news." The stranger went on to say that the Messiah had been born in Bethlehem. The young boy vaguely remembered hearing Isaiah's prophecy that someday the Messiah would come; but he had no idea what that meant. As he was trying to grasp what the stranger was talking about, the skies seemed to light up, and he could hear voices singing, "Glory to God in the highest."

What was going on? One of the elder shepherds said, "Let's go to Bethlehem and check this out." The boy started to turn away, for his father had entrusted him with the care of the sheep. But the elder shepherd said to him,

"Come along with us. The sheep will be alright, and your father will want a first-hand account of what we see." And so it was that the young boy on his first night as a shepherd was one of the first to arrive in Bethlehem and find Mary and Joseph and the Child lying in the manger. As he rushed home to tell his father the amazing news, he found his heart nearly bursting with joy, and he began to sing the song he had heard coming from the night sky.

Have you ever wondered why the first to learn about the most significant event in human history were the least significant people? Shepherds were uneducated ruffians, the lowest class of society. Not only were they the first to hear of the Messiah's birth, but they were the ones who were told that the birth meant "peace on earth." One might have expected the religious authorities to have been the first to be told the Good News. But there is an old saying that "war is too important to be left to the generals." And apparently God felt that the new "peace on earth" represented by the Christ child's birth was far too important to be left to the religious leaders and scholars who might draw conclusions based on their own perceptions and expectations of a Messiah. God bypassed the professional peacemakers and gave the message and its interpretation to amateurs.

Even today you and I associate "peace" as something our Secretary of State travels all over the world attempting to negotiate. Yet this new "peace on earth" does not depend upon North Korea stopping its threats to launch a nuclear missile. This peace is not about Israel and Palestine signing a truce or Syria and Afghanistan laying down their weapons. This peace which the angel proclaimed begins, not with nations and treaties and truces, but with individuals making peace first with God and then making peace with one's neighbors. The "peace which surpasses human understanding" is the change in human lives which begins with the change in human hearts.

This morning's Gospel concludes by telling us that the shepherds returned home. They returned to their ordinary lives – to cold, lonely nights in the desert watching their sheep. But now they were different. Their hearts were now filled with God's glory; their voices resounded in praise. They were changed by what they had seen and by what they had heard. Will that be true for you and me this morning? Will we be changed by all that we have heard and seen this Christmas? Will we still be filled with praise and glory for God when the excitement of Christmas is over: the dishes done, the decorations put away, the tree taken down? Will this Christmas - this celebration of the birth of the Christ child - bring about a change in our lives when we go back to work, back to school, back to our everyday routines? Like the shepherds of old, will our hearts still be filled with the wonder of the Christ child? Will you and I leave here today, our lives filled with worship and praise, discipleship and service?

"Peace on earth" begins by taking the events we have heard and seen into our hearts. And then, joining with those first shepherds and all the heavenly hosts, our hearts will also proclaim: "Glory to God in the highest and peace to God's people on earth."

Christmas morning 2012

The Changes a Baby Makes

This year (2007) our family has been blessed with four new babies. I have a new grand-nephew, two new grand-nieces, and a new great-granddaughter. As I participated in the excitement of waiting for these new babies and the joy of each baby's safe arrival, I was reminded of what a momentous event the birth of a new baby is in the life of a family. With the arrival of a new baby, whether a first child or a child who joins siblings, life in a family is forever changed. I remarked to my grandson and his wife as they were preparing excitedly for the birth of their first child after almost five years of marriage, "That baby is really going to change your life."

And when we think about how a baby changes so dramatically the life of a family, we can only imagine the impact of a royal birth - what happens when an heir to a throne is born. In that case, not just lives of the royal family are changed, but also the lives of every family in that nation, and the entire nation itself and its future may be forever changed.

The birth of a royal baby was probably the original setting for our first lesson. This morning's familiar reading from Isaiah (*Isaiah 9:2-7*) probably dates back to the 8th century B.C.E. Isaiah's prophecy was originally written in the form of a poem that was either part of the coronation ritual of a particular Judean King or else written for the festivities that accompanied the birth of a new crown prince. As we read Isaiah's prophecy for the impending royal birth, there seem to be three important and distinct predictions: The birth would be a sign of God's deliverance of the people from their oppressors; the birth would signal an era of justice and peace as the destruction of the gear of battle is described; and finally, Isaiah recognized that life for the people of Israel would be forever changed. And since Isaiah predicted that this change would be for the better, the prophecy persisted beyond its original purpose and became the symbol of hope for the people of Israel. Someday a Child would be born who would be called "Wonderful Counselor" because he would have wisdom to do what was right; he would be called "Mighty God" because he would have the power to accomplish God's deliverance of the people; he would be called "Everlasting Father" because he would be like a father to the nation, acting always for the welfare of his subjects whom he would regard as his children; and finally, he would be the "Prince of Peace" because his reign would inaugurate a time of peace and justice. The final verse of Isaiah's poem announces that this reign would come about, not through human effort, but by God's grace.

And so this morning's lesson becomes both a prediction and a description of the future Messiah for God's chosen people. And for generations the people of Israel waited and hoped and prepared for the day when this Messiah would come.

And then one day in a manger in the little town of Bethlehem, the long-awaited Messiah was born. Luke records the familiar facts of the birth - the birth of Jesus to a couple named Mary and Joseph. This was at last the child whom the prophet Isaiah had predicted: "To us a child is born, to us a son is given." And in keeping with Isaiah's prophecy the people knew that with the coming of the Messiah, their lives would be forever changed. This baby, if he were indeed the Messiah, thought the people, would reign as a mighty King, freeing the people from their oppressors and establishing justice and righteousness and peace.

The people of Israel expected their lives to be changed by the Messiah's birth, but they were quite mistaken as to how this Messiah would change their lives. Isaiah had predicted that "the people who walked in darkness have seen a great light." What the Jews didn't realize was that seeing that light would be quite different from recognizing just how that light would change the lives of humankind forever.

Within the familiar story that Luke portrays of the Christ child's birth, he records some quite different reactions to this Good News. A number of the Jewish leaders simply didn't believe that a child born in a manger to such unremarkable parents could be the long-awaited Messiah. King Herod and the Romans in authority felt threatened by someone who might unite the Jewish people against them. The shepherds, who were considered both low class and powerless, were at first terrified by the news; but their fears soon gave way to amazement and the decision to go and see for themselves.

You and I are here this morning because we believe the story. But do our songs of joy reflect the reality that our lives have been forever changed by this miraculous birth?

Today is Christmas. Amidst the family gatherings, the presents to be shared, the food and festivities, we are among millions of believers throughout the world who have gathered once again to celebrate the birth of the long-awaited Messiah. We relive in our worship today the event that forever changed God's relationship with humankind and humankind's relationship with God. We echo the herald angels as we sing, "Glory to the newborn King." We rejoice and acclaim with the shepherds of old: "Joy to the world! the Savior reigns."

But our celebration goes beyond proclaiming the birth of the Christ child into the world. For we recognize that when the baby Jesus came into the world, the whole world (including you and me) was forever changed.

As we gather to celebrate this new life of the Christ child, our true joy comes in the celebration of the new life offered to each of us by Jesus' birth. The anticipation is over. The new baby has been born. The day of joy is upon us. Isaiah's prophecy has come to pass. The Wonderful Counselor, Mighty God, Everlasting Father, Prince of Peace, has been born. God is now forever with us, and we are forever changed. Thanks be to God!

Christmas morning 2007

God's Priceless Gift

(And our Family's
Christmas Tradition)

In the small town of Ottawa, Illinois, where my mother was born and raised, as long as my family can remember a life-sized manger is always erected several weeks before Christmas on the town square in front of the courthouse. Choirs gather around the manger to sing Christmas carols and distribute cookies and hot cider before proceeding to serenade residents of the local nursing home. In years when it snows, one can often observe the tracks of children's sleds around the manger; and on more than one occasion a small child has been seen wandering into the scene and becoming part of it. The manger is not only at the center of this small town, it is the focal point for the town's celebration of Christmas. I have always thought that it would be difficult for the people of Ottawa to forget the true meaning of Christmas with the Christmas story staring so prominently at every shopper and passer-by.

A manger, which our family has always called by its French name "crèche," was also a prominent part of my own family's Christmas tradition. When I was a young child, the family crèche was from the Holy Lands, each figure hand-carved from the olive wood of that region. The crèche had been brought back from the Holy Lands by my grandparents, who had made a trip there in 1934, the summer I was born. Carrying on the tradition, I, too, brought back crèches for my children when I traveled to the Holy Lands in 1984. But the crèche in my living room today is very special, because three sheep and two cows are from the original family crèche of my childhood.

Just before bedtime on Christmas Eve when I was a child, the family would gather around the crèche. The baby Jesus, who had been hidden away during Advent, would be placed in the manger. Then Dad would read the Gospel story we have just heard. We would then hear a mini homily in which we would be reminded that the most priceless gift we receive on Christmas morning is the gift that God gave to the world: his Son, Jesus. We children would be reminded that all the gifts we would open the next morning were means by which we remember God's love. Dad would also remind us that the gifts we give to others help spread our love, and also God's love, to others.

Here at St. Gregory's Church, we, too, erect a manger each year. Long ago before my time here, it was decided that the manger would not be out in the churchyard or in our parish hall, but it would be right here in front of the altar in the most prominent and important place in our church. We can't miss seeing it here while we worship, and its presence provides us with a visual image as we listen to the Christmas Gospel. Its position also reminds us that the birth of the Christ child, God's special gift to humankind, is central to our worship together this morning. And because Jesus is called "Emmanuel," which means "God with us," we are also reminded that God is indeed with us in a very special way each time we gather at the altar.

A number of you were here last Sunday for the children's annual Christmas pageant. Each year we watch the children of this parish re-enact the Christmas story, and we participate in the pageant by singing Christmas carols that also help tell this story. This year I was particularly moved by our children's re-enactment of Jesus' birth. Our children weren't just acting in a play;

they seemed to be experiencing the Gospel story and drawing us into the story as well.

In some ways Sunday's pageant was not too different from a typical Sunday morning for many of our youngest children. Beginning at age three, our children participate in a special experiential Christian formation program called the "Catechesis of the Good Shepherd." Unlike more traditional "Sunday School" programs, our children don't just hear Bible stories and memorize Bible verses in Sunday School. Each Sunday our children enter into a special sacred space called "the Atrium," where they experience firsthand the great teachings of Jesus and the worship traditions of the Church. They act out stories such as the Good Shepherd; they wash their hands in the water of baptism; they set their own altar table and prepare the bread and wine for the Eucharist. They can even put on special vestments made to fit their small bodies so that they can act out the roles of priest and deacon. From their earliest memories our children learn that Church is not just school on Sunday, it is living, participatory faith development.

And last Sunday's pageant was so special, so sacred, because our children entered into the great mystery they were recounting and drew us into the sacrament they were portraying.

I was particularly struck by how tenderly the boy who portrayed Joseph and the girl who was Mary held the real baby who was Jesus. It was as if we were eavesdropping on the new parents. The young girl held the young baby so carefully in her arms and looked at him with such awe and wonder that I could only think that must have been the way in which the first Mary gazed upon her baby, the Christ child. And the young baby slept throughout the entire pageant - "no crying he made." His angelic sleeping face could not have portrayed a more realistic Prince of Peace. The children acting as the stars and wise men, the angels and archangel, the sheep and shepherds, seemed to be living the true meaning of the Gospel story they were re-enacting. Our children knew that the baby Jesus was the gift of God's love, and so they were able to convey that love to us in the wonderful event we simplistically call "the pageant."

In spite of a frantic shopping season that began even before Thanksgiving - a season that often seems most concerned with its effect on our nation's economy - I was struck this year by how often "love" was a recurring theme in so many of the TV commercials. Many advertisers emphasized how to find the priceless gift to express our love for that special person in our lives. And that of course is what God has done for us - given to each of us the "priceless" gift of love:

A silver BMW wrapped in a red ribbon - $34,800;

Play Station 3 - $610;

A diamond necklace - $199;

Jesus, the perfect gift from God to the people of God - priceless!

Christmas morning 2006

The Back Page News

My mother recently celebrated her ninety-fourth birthday. She is an amazing woman. Although her body is wearing out, her mind is as alert as ever, and she keeps very much up to date about the world beyond her retirement community. She stays informed about local, national, world, and Church politics, as well as her beloved Denver Broncos. Every single morning, she reads the Denver Post from cover to cover.

When I visited her recently, I watched closely as she performed her daily ritual of reading the newspaper. I noticed that she quickly skimmed the headlines and front-page stories. She glanced at the headlines as if they no longer held much interest for her, and I began to wonder if she was finally losing her ability to keep up with world events. But as she turned page after page, quickly skimming past the scandals, past the department store ads, her interest seemed to pick up until finally she reached the section of her paper that is comparable to our "Metro" section of the Tribune. I watched as she began to concentrate and study each article intensely. I asked her what was so interesting, and she said something very curious to me. She said, "The headlines aren't what's really important to me anymore; the real news is what's happening locally to my friends and neighbors." To my mother, what is happening to famous people and great world powers on the front page is not nearly as important as what is happening to the "local people" on the back page.

If there had been newspapers in the First Century, the front page each day would have been filled with news of Rome and Caesar

Augustus, who would have been hailed on the front pages as the "Prince of Peace" as he began to bring an end to the wars that were threatening the Roman Empire. Articles would have been written about all the statues and shrines that were being erected to him throughout the provinces of the Roman Empire. Caesar Augustus would always have been front page news, and the census that he had called for would also have been a major headline event. There would have been numerous reactions and letters to the editor about that forthcoming census. There would have been reports of town meetings and demonstrations being organized, for the Jews hated even the thought of a census. They still recalled with anger and sadness the census taken by King David to demonstrate his power - a census which had subsequently invoked God's wrath. And so like so many newspaper headlines, the Jews would have found the front page news to be "bad news" indeed.

But while the front page carried the same old bad news, the same old oppressor, and the same violent reactions to his decrees, on the back page happening almost unnoticed, a very different kind of story was noted - the news of a savior's birth - a birth of one who would teach the world a whole new way of living and being in relationship to the creator. Like my mother, Luke in writing his Gospel seems to be aware of the headline events, but he draws our attention to a local event on the back page.

That local event would have reported what had happened to a group of shepherds. Most of us have only a "Christmas pageant" concept of shepherds. And so we tend to romanticize that group of people in much the same way that we often hold on to an unrealistic picture of the American "cowboy." In reality shepherds were smelly, unruly, uneducated, "tough" men. They were often crooks or hustlers. A young woman wouldn't want to encounter a shepherd alone on a dark night. And so a part of the story that we don't hear about is that Mary may well have been terrified when those ruffians walked through the stable door in the middle of the night! But Mary soon learned that they meant no harm. They had come to verify what they had been told by an angel. Those rough and unruly men had come to ask Mary, "Is your baby the one for whom everyone has been waiting? Is your baby the one who will bring peace to this world and good will among all people?" "Do you think," the shepherds would have asked Mary, "that your baby is the One?" Luke tells us that Mary listened to those unlikely bearers of glad tidings, and when the shepherds had left to return to their flocks, Mary kept wondering about what they had said. Luke tells us that she kept pondering what she had been told in her heart.

It's no accident that Luke chose to report the story of the shepherds. Luke's entire Gospel is like the back pages of a local newspaper. Luke sees history from the point of view of the forgotten, the downtrodden, the woebegone; the poor people whom Jesus says will always be with us; the people no one pays any attention to. The shepherds' presence reminds us that when God acts in this world, God acts through the "ordinary people," people whom society may not think are very important - people who only make back page news. But Luke suggests that you and I better pay attention to the stories of what happens to "ordinary people," for it is through those ordinary peoples' lives - lives like yours and mine - that God acts in the world.

And so here we are two thousand years later, and the front page headlines still carry bad news; and the Good News which we celebrate today is still only a back page story.

There are millions of people who still have not heard the story, so it's up to us, the ordinary people, to tell the story to those who have not heard it; to proclaim to the whole world the

Good News: to us has been born the Savior, who is Christ the Lord. Alleluia!

Christmas morning 2004

My mother, Mary Palmer Woods, passed away December 12, 2006, so this homily is dedicated to her memory, and to provide a story for the youngest generations of the Woods family to remember her.

The Light Observed

Signs and symbols, reminding us that Christmas is coming, have surrounded us for weeks: Christmas trees, the Salvation Army bell ringers in front of Jewel, shoppers buying presents for family and friends, the smell of turkey cooking or cookies baking, *It's a Wonderful Life* on TV, the parties, the gatherings with family. But those events are only the reminders. Christmas is really about the story, the very special story about that time so long ago when God gave the world the gift of his Son. It is the story of when the Light of Christ came into the world.

The Christmas story begins one silent night very long ago, a night when suddenly everything lit up and became bright. Mary has wrapped the baby tightly and is holding him close to her body to keep him warm in the drafty barn. Joseph has made them a comfortable bed of straw, but Mary gets up and moves toward the stable's doorway. Light is streaming in as if it were daylight. She is perplexed: it couldn't be morning already. And then she sees the source of the brightness. There is a star in the night sky that is brighter than the moon. She calls Joseph over to the doorway. He stands beside her and puts his arm around his family as together they gaze into the night - the holy night. Joseph is the first to speak. "I've never seen that star before. It's as if God is shining a special light upon us." Mary replies, "I wonder if God wants the world to know the Christ child has come into the world."

But it is not just the stable that is covered with light. The usually dark streets of the village have become bathed in light, as the sky becomes bright as noonday. By now all of Bethlehem is beginning to stir. Babies begin to cry, thinking it is time to be fed; donkeys bray; the roosters' cries are awakening the chickens. A small child becomes fearful of the noise and goes to her father., "Is something bad happening?" The father gathers his daughter into his arms and begins to think about the prophet's words - words that said when the Messiah comes, a light would shine on those who lived in darkness. The prophet had said that when this happened, life for the people of Israel would change; for a child would be born to the people, a child who would be "Wonderful Counselor, Mighty God, Everlasting Father, Prince of Peace." The father hugs his daughter closely as he shakes his head in wonderment: "I'm not sure what is happening, but I think it must be something good – something very good." And so the village father and his young daughter are among the first to recognize the Light of Christ.

This heavenly light begins to shine so brightly it can be seen clear into the desert where shepherds are watching their flocks. The young boy rubs his hands as he tries to stay warm in the desert night. He has built a fire and is surprised at how much light the fire seems to be giving off. And then he realizes that the night has become so bright he can see his uncle's campfire in the distance. Other shepherds have gathered around Uncle's campfire, and they seem to be talking to a stranger. The boy decides that something is going on. He hurries toward his uncle in time to hear the stranger say, "Do not be afraid, for see, I am bringing you good news." His uncle turns to him and says, "Something is happening. Secure the sheep. We must follow the star and see where it is leading us." And so the shepherds follow the Light of Christ to the manger in Bethlehem.

Soon the news of Jesus' birth begins to spread far and wide, and by the light of that same star we are told that wise men would come from far off to pay homage to the Christ child. This part of the story is of particular importance to you and me, for it signifies that the Christ child was to be a light, not just for the people of Israel, but for all people everywhere. The Light of Christ came into the world for you and for me.

And so once again we hear the Christmas story. The Light of Christ has come into the world: the Light of Christ which first lit up the night sky in Bethlehem on that holy night; the Light of Christ which proclaimed the Savior's birth. And now it is up to you and me to keep the Light of Christ burning brightly, and to tell the world the good news of great joy: "Unto us a child is born; oh come, let us adore him."

And so on this day we become part of the Christmas story as we join with the angels and archangels, the shepherds and the villagers, in proclaiming: *"The Light of Christ has come into the world."*

Christmas morning 2013

To us a Child is Born

It was a cold, gloomy, wet winter day. I was at the hospital, sitting at the bedside of a woman who was quite ill and in obvious pain. Her brows were knit with worry and anxiety: anxiety about her health, worry about the burden of deciding her course of treatment, and concern about her future. I sat there wondering what to say: what words of comfort, what words of hope, what words of peace I might offer. And then I heard a sound (*Brahms' Lullaby begins to play in the background*). Not realizing where the music was coming from, my first thought was, "That's a very strange choice for a mobile phone ringtone." But then as I looked over at the woman, I saw that her whole demeanor had changed: she was smiling; she looked more relaxed; she seemed suddenly at peace. We sat quietly for a few minutes. And then the music began again. The woman began to laugh out loud as she exclaimed, "It must be a busy day on the obstetrics ward." Then I realized that the lullaby was being played over the hospital loudspeaker whenever a new baby was born.

What a joyous thing for the hospital to do! Every newborn baby should be so welcomed into the world, for the birth of every new baby is always a momentous event. There is preparation and anticipation for the parents-to-be. There is excitement and joy when the baby is finally born.

And there is also the realization that life has been forever changed by the arrival of this new life in one's midst. My sick friend's response to the announcement of a new baby's birth was somewhat different from that of the child's parents, for the announcement brought her hope and comfort, assurance and peace.

So it was with the people of Israel. At the time of our first lesson from Isaiah, the Jews had seen their city and temple destroyed. They had wandered for years in exile, and they had become convinced that God had not only abandoned their Holy City, but God had also abandoned the chosen people. And so the Israelites greeted the news of an impending royal birth with joy and expectation. They were comforted by the prophet's assurance that this birth would be a sign of God's deliverance from their oppressors. Isaiah told them that this birth would usher in an era of justice and peace; this new birth would change the lives of the Israelites forever. It is no wonder that this prophecy prophesy of a royal birth became interpreted by the people of Israel to be a prediction of a Savior, a Messiah, who would come to save the people.

And so this prophecy of Isaiah became a symbol of hope for the Israelites. Someday a child would be born who would be called

"Wonderful Counselor" because he would have wisdom to do what was right; he would be called "Mighty God" because he would deliver the people from their oppressors; he would be called "Everlasting Father" because he would be like a parent to the nation, acting always for the welfare of his children, the Israelites; and he would be the "Prince of Peace" because his reign would inaugurate a time of peace and justice for the people of Israel. And so for generations the Israelites waited and hoped and prepared for the day that Isaiah's prophecy would come true - the day that the Messiah would be born.

Then one day in a manger in the little town of Bethlehem the long-awaited Messiah was born. The prophecy of Isaiah had at last come true: "To us a child is born, to us a son is given." Luke records the familiar facts of the birth: the baby Jesus was born to a couple named Mary and Joseph. This baby, if he were indeed the Messiah, would reign as a mighty King, freeing the people from their oppressors and establishing justice and righteousness and peace.

The Israelites expected their lives to be changed by the Messiah's birth, but they were quite mistaken as to how this Messiah would change their lives. Isaiah had predicted that "the people who walked in darkness have seen a great light." But the Israelites misinterpreted the meaning of the light, and so they didn't understand how God was calling them to respond to that light.

How did the people of that day respond to the child's birth? In our Gospel this morning Luke describes several quite different reactions to this Good News. The Jewish leaders couldn't imagine that a child born in a manger to such unremarkable parents could be the long-awaited Messiah, and so their response was disbelief. King Herod and the Romans in authority, fearing that the baby might unite the Jewish people against them, were threatened by the news, and so they responded with fearful aggression. The shepherds, who were considered both low class and powerless, were terrified by the news at first, but their fears gave way to amazement; and so they responded by going to see for themselves.

And what about you and me today? What do we make of this familiar story? Signs and symbols of Christmas have surrounded us for weeks: Christmas trees, endless ads to entice shoppers, an influx of greeting cards from family and friends, gifts to be bought and received, Christmas cookies, fudge. But do any of those signs of Christmas point to Jesus' birth? Does Christmas remind us that Jesus' birth changed our lives and those of all humankind forever?

The woman in the hospital told me that each time she heard the lullaby announce the birth of a new baby, she was reminded of the baby Jesus. The musical announcement of a new birth became for her like the star over Bethlehem. It pointed her to Jesus and brought her comfort and peace in the midst of her pain and anxiety.

How do we respond to the birth of the Christ child? Does Christmas make a difference in our lives? (*Brahms's Lullaby begins to play*) "To us a child is born, to us a son is given; and the government will be upon his shoulders; and his name will be called Wonderful Counselor, Mighty God, Everlasting Father, Prince of Peace."

Christmas morning 2014

The Cosmic Christmas Story

As the theme from the movie Stars Wars *is heard, the preacher steps down to the Crossing and begins:*

"A long time ago in a galaxy far, far away." These words and music set the stage for the Star Wars trilogy, beginning with the first episode, titled *A New Hope*, in which the young boy, Luke Skywalker, and Han Solo, captain of the Millennium Falcon, work together with the companionable droid duo, R2-D2 and C-3PO, to rescue the beautiful princess Leia, and help the Rebel Alliance restore freedom and justice to the Galaxy. It is the story of the struggle between good and evil, between light and darkness. And now in theaters everywhere this season, there is a new *Star Wars* movie - a kind of prequel that comes before and sets the context for the familiar first Trilogy - a movie that takes us back to the beginning before the beginning of *Star Wars*.

This morning's Gospel sounds more like a scene from *Star Wars* than the Christmas story. When we think of the Christmas story what usually comes to mind is the story portrayed by Luke's account of Jesus' birth and enacted by our children in last Sunday's pageant. It would be hard for our Church school children to make a pageant out of this morning's Gospel. There is no mention of Mary and Joseph searching for lodging - no description of a baby born in a barn. There is no talk of angels or wise men following a star to Bethlehem. It has a *Star Wars*-like theme with light overcoming darkness. And like the new *Stars Wars* movie, it too is a prequel that comes before and sets the context for the more familiar story. And yet this morning's

Gospel IS the Christmas story. It is the COSMIC Christmas story.

John's setting is not the little town of Bethlehem; John's setting is the whole universe. John doesn't begin his story when Quirinius was governor of Syria; John takes us back to the beginning - to the very beginning - even before the beginning. John's account takes us back to creation. Andrew Daughters, a poet and Episcopal priest, paraphrased this morning's gospel with his poem:

"In the beginning, before the beginning, without a beginning was God.
He made the beginning; he was the beginning, creating creation was God." *

John takes us all the way back to creation, and when we reread the creation story in Genesis, we encounter that same phrase used by John: "In the beginning . . ." We are told that in that beginning, there was only God and the Word of God and the Breath of God.

John tells us that in the beginning - in that beginning before the heavens and the earth were even brought into being - the Word was there. The Word always was. When we hear "the Word," we think of speech and language: how we express our thoughts and our feelings. We think of the power that our words have over us and others. Angry, destructive, cutting words: "I hate you." "You're stupid." Tender, healing, affirming words: "Congratulations." "I love you."

But when John speaks of "The Word," he is taking us far beyond what we can imagine in terms of human language or articulation. John is taking us to the awesome, creative utterance of God when all existence was called into being by God. John's Jewish audience would have understood that it was this same Word of God which had blessed Jacob; this same Word of God which had called Abraham out of his familiar surroundings. John's Greek audience would have understood this Word of God to be the divine *Logos*, the Reason or Mind of God.

And John tells us that this Word became human and came to live among us; and so at Christmas we give this Word the name Jesus. Our Gospel goes on to say that this Word, Jesus, was the light of all people: the light that overcame the darkness. You and I have been given that light - that same power - to overcome the darkness of this world.

Our youngest children here at St. Gregory's have been taught what it means for them to be Christ's light in the world. At the Easter Eve Service of Water and Light, our children are reminded that they received the power to be Christ's light in the world at their baptism. And as they renew the promises made at their baptism when they first received the Light of Christ, each child receives a lighted candle and responds, "I am the light of Christ." That is not just the baptismal message; that is the true Christmas message.

Each of us here today has been empowered by the Word made flesh to be Christ's light in the world. We have been given the power to overcome the darkness of the world: the darkness of poverty and starvation, the darkness of war and terrorism and violence, the darkness of hatred and prejudice; the darkness that invades human lives.

Much of the world may not know or be able to understand the impact of a baby born long ago in humble circumstances in a remote village called Bethlehem. But when the Light of Christ shines through us into the world, the world will come to know the meaning of Christmas. To be the Light of Christ in the world is to proclaim to the world that we are all God's creation; that we all belong to God; that we are all loved by God. To be the Light of Christ in the world is to tell the world that the God who created us loved us enough to become "flesh and blood and move into our neighborhood."

And so as we celebrate Christmas this morning, let us participate in the Cosmic Christmas. Let us become Christ's light in the world. Perhaps that old familiar hymn, "I want to walk as a child of the light" might become our Cosmic Christmas carol.

* Andrew Daughters. *A Gospel Treasury, (Lima, Ohio: C.S.S. Publishing Company, Inc., 1988), p.20.*

Christmas morning 2016

First published as
Christmas Retold: Stories of Christmas
© 2021 Meredith Woods Potter.
Original cover (above) by Carolyn (Casey) Kremer.

Acknowledgements
to the first edition

My gratitude to Carolyn (Casey) Kremer, Director of Communications, St. Gregory's Episcopal Church, Deerfield, Illinois for designing the cover for this book and for taking the photograph of the family crèche and incorporating it in the cover design of the first edition. Thanks to my dear friend, Carol Harper, for encouraging me to undertake this project and for her editorial counsel. And I am ever grateful to the beloved members of St. Gregory's Church who have been such supportive and attentive listeners to my sermons over the years.

About the Author

Meredith Woods Potter is well known for her insightful and knowledgeable sermons. People have said that they would check the Sunday schedule to be sure they wouldn't miss out when she was preaching. Her preaching is enriched by unique life experiences: spending her childhood years in a foreign country, being a single mother of four boys, serving as a college math professor, feeling the call to ordained ministry as a second vocation before women were even being ordained in the Episcopal Church, and being assigned to a Korean congregation as her first placement. Her sermons are solidly based in scripture and study, but her style is personal and speaks directly to her hearers. Her willingness to take the Christmas morning services for so many years attests to her dedication to having families center Christmas in Christ. She continues to enrich her study of the faith by studying Hebrew in her retirement!